FROM THE LITTLEST TO THE BIGGEST!

ANIMAL BOOK 4 YEARS OLD

Children's Animal Books

BABY PROFESSOR

EDUCATION KIDS

Speedy Publishing LLC
40 E. Main St. #1156
Newark, DE 19711
www.speedypublishing.com
Copyright 2017

In this book, we're going to talk about some of the littlest and biggest animals on Earth. So, let's get right to it!

No one really knows how many species of animals there are on our planet. Over 10,000 new species are found every year. Some scientists say there are 2 million species. Others say that there could be more than 50 million!

Some animals are really big, even bigger than a school bus. Other animals are so small you can hold them in the palm of your hand. Since new animals are being found

Bog Turtle

all the time, there may be some smaller ones that scientists don't know about yet. Maybe you'll grow up to be a scientist and discover new species!

AMPHIBIANS

Amphibians are cold-blooded animals that have skeletons. Frogs, newts, toads, and salamanders are all amphibians. The biggest amphibian on Earth is the Chinese giant salamander. They are over 6 feet long and live in the waterways of China.

Panamanian golden frog

Giant Salamander

Unfortunately, these interesting animals are on the endangered species list. One of the reasons is that they are used for medicines. Also, air and water pollution has a big effect on them and their habitats.

These salamanders have terrible eyesight so they sense movement to hunt for things to eat. Like many types of amphibians, they need to have a watery home but sometimes come up on land. The female Chinese giant salamander lays over 500 eggs at one time. The male salamanders help the females watch over the eggs. Even though these animals are very big, they are gentle giants.

The littlest amphibian on Earth was just found in 2012. It's a tiny frog that lives in New Guinea. It's only 0.27 inches long and it can fit on half the surface of a dime. It's so tiny! These frogs were making sounds like insects and that is how scientists found them. They live in moist leaves in the forest.

Paedophryne Amauensis

Corn Spider

SPIDERS

Spiders are not insects. They are arachnids. They have eight legs and an exoskeleton. Lots of people are afraid of spiders. The biggest one on Earth is pretty scary.

It's called the goliath birdeater tarantula. It lives in the northern part of South America. It can get as big as a foot across and its fangs measure up to 2 inches long! It captures mice, frogs, and worms to eat.

Goliath Bird Eater Tarantula

Despite its name, it doesn't eat birds very often though it's big enough that it could. These spiders are known to make hissing sounds when they are threatened. They also send out barbed hairs like tiny spears in the air if they're attacked.

The littlest spider on Earth is the incredibly small patu digua. It lives on moss in Western Samoa. It's so tiny that it fits on the head of a pin about 0.37 millimeters wide. Believe it or not this tiny spider actually spins a web to catch its food.

Osprey

BIRDS

Birds are warm-blooded animals that have skeletons. They have feathers, wings, and beaks. Most birds are also able to fly.

The biggest bird on Earth is the ostrich. It's about 9 feet tall and can weigh around 350 pounds. It has the biggest egg in the world that weighs in at 3 pounds. Even though it's big and doesn't fly, it can run really fast—over 60 miles per hour.

Ostrich

Bee Hummingbird

The littlest bird on Earth is a type of hummingbird called the bee hummingbird. It's found in Cuba. It's so tiny that you might think it's an insect when it's flying around. It's only about 2 inches long from beak to tail. It beats its wings so fast that only high-speed cameras are able to capture a photo of it! Its nest is only 1.2 inches wide.

FISH

Fish are cold-blooded animals that have skeletons. Some fish have skeletons that are made of cartilage. Cartilage is more flexible than bone. Fish live underwater and have gills to breathe.

Clown fish

The biggest fish on Earth is the whale shark. This huge shark is over 40 feet long. It weighs about 47,000 pounds. Luckily, this huge creature isn't dangerous to people unless it runs into a boat. It doesn't eat fish. Instead, it

eats plankton. It just opens its mouth wide and swims along as the water goes in. It filters out the plankton in the water to eat. It's amazing that such a large creature can eat enough plankton to stay alive.

The littlest fish on Earth is a teeny tiny fish with a big scientific name, Paedocypris progenetica. It has a see-through body and no skeleton in its head. It's only .31 inches long, which is about the same size as a mosquito. It was found in Indonesia in 2006. It's amazing that this little fish has a backbone just like a normal-size fish.

Potato Beetle

INSECTS

Insects are small animals that have no skeletons. They have six legs and usually they have one or two pairs of wings.

The biggest insect on Earth is a stick insect that was found in southern China in 2016. It is 24.6 inches long! It's not the heaviest insect though. That insect is the giant weta cricket. Recently, a giant weta cricket was found that weighs three times as much as a mouse.

Stick Insect

The littlest insects on Earth are called fairyflies. They are tiny wasps. Even though they are only 0.139 millimeters long, their bodies have a way to breathe, a way to eat, and a way to reproduce.

Fairyfly

American Bison

MAMMALS

Mammals are warm-blooded animals that have skeletons. They usually have hair or fur. They usually give birth to live young and are fed milk by their mothers. Humans are mammals.

Blue Whale

The biggest mammal on Earth is the blue whale. You might think that the blue whale is a fish. It doesn't have hair or fur like many other mammals. This enormous animal gives birth to a baby whale that is 25 feet when it's just born! It's fed its mother's milk until it gets full grown. When it's an adult, it will be about 98 feet long and will weigh 180 metric tons. The blue whale needs to eat about 7,900 pounds of small shrimp called krill every day. It needs to eat about 1.5 million calories every day.

African Elephant

The blue whale lives in the ocean. There are also some large mammals that live on land. The largest land mammal is the African elephant and the next largest is the Asian elephant. The largest African elephant ever measured was about 13 feet tall.

ts weight was 24,000 pounds. It wouldn't be good to have an elephant for a pet. You would have to feed it over 400 pounds of food every day. You'd also have to find 30 gallons of fresh water for it to drink!

Etruscan Shrew

There are two animals that win for the littlest mammal on Earth. One of the animals is the Etruscan shrew. Shrews are small mammals that are like moles. This type of shrew weighs less than two grams and is only about 2.3 inches long.

Even though these animals are small, they like to eat a lot! They eat twice the weight of their bodies every single day. They have very fast heartbeats. Their hearts beat around 1500 times per minute. Human hearts beat about 75 beats per minute. Another very small mammal is the tiny bumblebee bat that lives in Thailand. It has a wingspan of 5 inches and would easily fit in the palm of your hand. It's about the same weight as a quarter.

REPTILES

Reptiles are cold-blooded animals that have skeletons. They usually have dry skin with scales and lay eggs on land. Snakes, turtles, crocodiles, and alligators are examples of reptiles.

The biggest reptiles on Earth are saltwater crocodiles, also called "salties." The largest one on record was over 20 feet long and weighed 3,000 pounds. It is one of the world's most dangerous creatures. A saltwater crocodile will stay near the edge of the water to watch animals or people. Once it decides it is ready, it jumps out of the water, and drags the animal or person underwater.

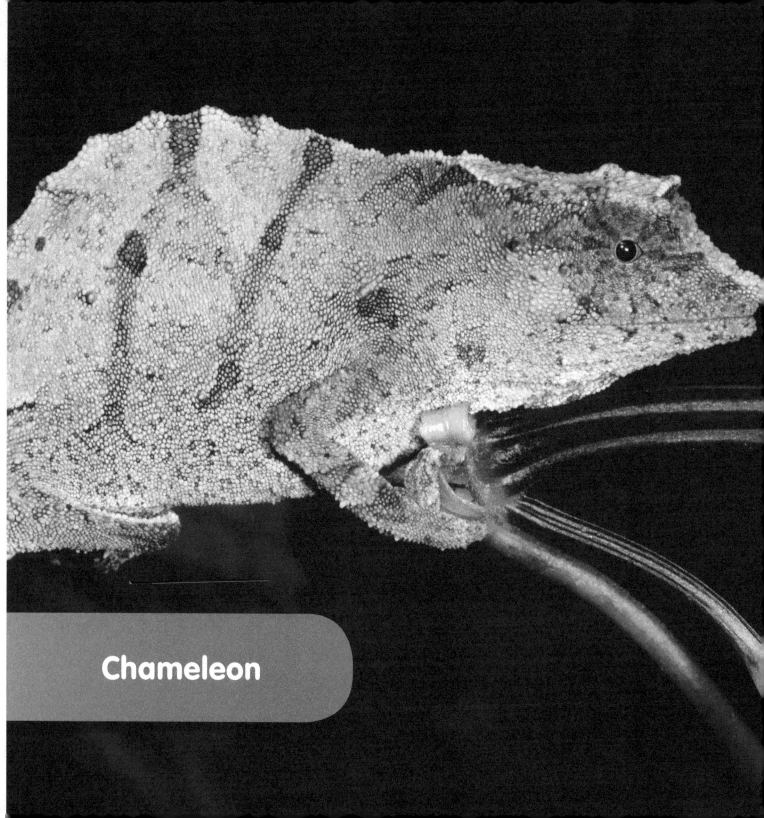

Chameleon

The littlest reptile on Earth is a very tiny type of chameleon from Madagascar. These lizards are so small that even one that's reached adult size can fit on the head of a match. They were found on a small island named Nosy Hara. Scientists believe that this animal is a case of island dwarfism. Animals that live on islands sometimes get smaller and smaller over time, because they have less food to choose from.

MICROBES

There are some animals on our planet that are so small we can't even see them. These are microscopic creatures in our soil and water. There are billions in just one teaspoon of soil or water!

Awesome! Now you know more about all the interesting littlest and biggest animals on Earth. You can find more Animals books from Baby Professor by searching the website of your favorite book retailer.

Visit

BABY PROFESSOR
EDUCATION KIDS

www.BabyProfessorBooks.com

to download Free Baby Professor eBooks
and view our catalog of new and exciting
Children's Books

CPSIA information can be obtained
at www.ICGtesting.com
Printed in the USA
LVHW061001070922
727785LV00012B/97